LIBERATION
OF FEAR AND LOVE

A Collection of Poetry

*Thanks for your
support! I hope
my words can serve
as a great inspiration to
you!*

Christopher

CHRISTOPHER GASKINS

Library of Congress Control Number: 2012905135
ISBN: Hardcover   978-1-4691-8695-5
                Softcover   978-1-4691-8694-8
                Ebook   978-1-4691-8696-2

Photography by Tia Hall

Cover Illustration by Sebastian Caceres

This book was printed in the United States of America.

To order additional copies of this book, contact:
Xlibris Corporation
1-888-795-4274
www.Xlibris.com
Orders@Xlibris.com
111012

CONTENTS

SECTION II: THE METRONOME OF LOVE AND MUSIC

Acknowledgments

To God: My will is to satisfy your will through my passion to help others. I now understand that this is my purpose in life while I am here on this earth. Please continue to give me strength. I thank you for the joy of life.

To my mother and father: Thank you both for always being such a strong support system and motivators in my life. I love you both very much.

Special thanks to Tia Hall and Sebastian Caceres for giving my words vision and life in the form of photography and art. Much respect.

PROLOGUE

I truly believe love is the panacea for all of the world's ills and pains. Love. Yes, just love. First you must liberate fear in order to liberate love. It is through love that compassion and understanding are discovered. Understand the stories of the impoverished, the minority, the abused, and the brokenhearted. Understand the stories of the faithful and spiritual, the optimist and the fearless lover. Understand the rhythm of the musician who speaks in harmony. Dare to dream like the dreamer who strives every day to make reality and dreams become one . . .

SECTION I

PERSPECTIVES BEYOND THE VEIL

Africa, it is deceit!

The sun brings light to the flame of her dreams.

Homeless man, please lend me your keys.

If only I could walk in the dark with certainty that luminous rays will always light my path.

We once walked as kings amongst pyramids in Africa.
Now some walk as kings of the ghetto.

BROKEN SILENCE
(PRELUDE)

It is time.
It is time for words to unravel
from the lines of these pages
and stand upright in the face of life.

It is time for my words to sprint
to the center of intellect and confusion,
grandeur and humility,
pain, suffering, and strife,
love and passion,
desire and rage—
straight to your heart, mind, and soul!

I am art!
Take form in the shape of the black fist,
an oak root in the earth,
the wings of eagles,
an open heart,
an open book,
a Bible with worn pages.
A sinner in the blood of Jesus.
A searching soul.

My mind thrives in the vitality of Socratic dialogue.
I resonate with the hush of the question
before the answer is whispered.
This is only the ocean's shore.
No longer shall I stare at the face of the water;
dive with me into the depths of my soul and heart.
I welcome you.

Christopher

Stick my aspirations on kites
and let them go wherever the wind blows.

Protect my dreams in cocoons
for they will one day turn into butterflies.

Plant my blessings in soil
so others can reap my harvest.

Allow my love to ascend infinitely
so humanity can ride on shooting stars.

Stick my scrolls of success in time capsules
so my grandchildren can learn from my experiences.

Savor my food for thought in these words
for they may one day fill empty stomachs of hungry children.

Sing my songs like birds serenade nature;
our songs can cleanse the air.

Remember my words,
for they are my way
of sticking messages in bottles and setting them out to sea
to never be forgotten,
but to be discovered in life's time
when skies are dark
to remind one,
miracles are possible.

MISUNDERSTOOD

Walking alone in crowded corridors,
communing in solace of confusion.
Sitting in coffee shops
sipping on green tea
steeping secrets in waters of catharses.

Stepping over medians of average
to examine poorly erased marks outside margins.
Utter riddles to riddle withered minds
In order to singe conceptions where no flame was ever lit.

Elevating to depths of cerebral diffusion,
sinking to heights below the summit
to submit.
To kneel on cold, cold sidewalks,
and outstretch arms to things unseen.

Embrace what's felt in private thoughts.
Envision yet reflect,
mirrors sometimes contort
and mirrors align truth.
For which is to be seen?

To scholars draped in robes of academia
or men with homes in alleys and forgotten blocks
who scribble on liquor-stained scrolls of ignored perspectives.
The answer is on the other side of the coin.

To be misunderstood
may be to unknowingly twirl on twines of insanity
with passions to plunge into depths of brilliance.
So bundle my thoughts in straitjackets
and cast them between adjoining walls.
To be misunderstood.

TO YOUNG MINDS

If I could blow away the clouds that clout their minds,
capture stormy rains in scores of mason jars,
summon rainbows into existence
or beckon sunlight into their lives,
I would.

When light didn't prevail,
I would release fireflies from cupped hands
when times were dark, to guide them,
to help them.
I would give words wings and let my love soar
en route to their minds and hearts.

Would they listen?

In the Rough
(Two stories far apart, yet so similar)

A young prodigy is in the streets of an American metropolis—
     A rare diamond is lost in the nature of Sierra Leone—
hidden under the darkness of broken streetlights
     hidden under the muck and mire
within a concrete jungle's twisted vines
     within reach of a boy soldier's calloused hands.
and between a dollar and a dream.
     A jewel of immense worth.
A prodigy is lost and
     A diamond in the rough
is in need of guidance and nurturing.
     is in need of refinement and polishing.
Entrenched in milieus full of grime
     Entrenched in milieus full of grime
exists something that shines so bright
     exists something that shines so bright
that it is blinding.
     that it is blinding.
So we do not see it.
     So we do not see it.
Yet, we comb the earth in search of what is near.
     Still, the diamond in the rough awaits discovery.

LISTEN BROTHA

I extend my hand and you extend yours
interlock fingers
symbolic of a bond of trust.

Ask for my promise
and I give you my word;
take away your trust
and you take away your cornerstone;
take away your moral value
and you take away your worth.

As a man,
these are sometimes the only things we have.
Display superior conduct.
Enforce excellence in spite of immoral impotence
because you see,
a sentence for assisting in filling these vials of emptiness
with half-empty cups of desolation
is to leave the cup of opportunity only halfway full
and this, my friend,
is more time than life has to spare.

BLACK MAN

If Michelangelo were to draw a portrait of the African American man,
he would have needed more colors of paint than just that of a Moor.
Only a collage would be fit—
created with a brush of many threads
to capture a background of rich cultures,
a sky with clouds of many faces
and grounds imprinted with footprints
traveling in different directions.

We once walked as kings amongst pyramids.
Now some walk as kings of the ghetto;
some pace in cells where no light shines.
Many walk through gates of prestigious universities.
Some run down fields toward end zones;
Others, toward bases, nets, and finish lines
aggressively toward the goal to become "champion."
Some waltz down Wall Street,
on Capitol Hill
and into business meetings.
Many walk down the aisle and into the pulpit.

The complexion of a black man has a lot more diversity
than what is often portrayed.
The diaspora of life lies within our mixes of melanin,
so when asked how to define a black man, say,
"We represent the uniqueness of black sands on tropical islands,
the fire of the mountain
and the cool of the water.
We ARE."

WHEN WILL THE HEALING BE COMPLETE?

From castration in front of our ebony sisters
to rope from the neck to a sturdy limb on the old oak,
to rope around the ankles and wrists
bound to four horses running wild at the crack of the whip . . .

Our concept of family and manhood has been severed,
plaguing our women with scarred visions
that translate down generational lines.

They lost faith in us!
WE lost faith in us!
The confidence to be the kings that we were destined to be
is hidden on the floor of the Atlantic.
We search for our lost crowns
over three hundred years later.
We still search for healing
in the fatherless homes,
in the overpopulated jails,
on the streets littered with whisky bottles and beer cans,
in the dimly lit homeless shelters.

Will we ever excavate our destiny?
For the rape of our souls, we pray to be healed.
For the rape of our minds, we pray to be healed.
For the rape of our family, we pray to be healed.

Good Morning

I'm leaving an empty scroll
next to where you sleep at night,
so when you awake
and your eyes capture life the first moment after your slumber,
you will see opportunity.
Even when it doesn't stare back at you,
it is there.
It lies in the recesses of the imagination in the blank scroll.
Naked threads await to wed penetrating ink
To forge a life together forever.

Live to search for love!
Wince from pain;
laugh
cry
smile
mourn
rejoice.
Most of all, give thanks for a new day!

The journey lies in the recesses of this empty scroll.
Rediscover dreams in the ink of life;
The pen lays next to your heart and mind
and the ink waits to flow like water
through the mountains and valleys of your aspirations.
Today is another day to create your masterpiece . . .
Good morning!

INTERVIEW IN BLACK FACE

Sometimes I really want to drop out of school
come back as a media major
or a public relations major or something,
finish at the bottom of my class,
kiss ass in the industry
just so I can get an interview with the CEO of BET.
Show up on CP time
smacking on fried chicken,
spilling watermelon juice all over her desk,
spitting black seeds in the trash can,
floss ma' bling—
I mean swang ma' diamond—
I had meant swang ma' cubic zirconium-encrusted black sambo chain
ALL UP in that gurl's face!
Wipe dem grease stains off ma' lips,
pic chiken out ma' grill wit chiken bone toofpicks and ask her,
"Ya jus don't get it, do ya?"
And she'd reply with a smile, "You want cha sum hot sauce wit that bird,
boy?"

LYE AND DECEIT

European influence:
Africa ugly
Africa nappy
Africa charred black
Africa broad noses
Africa fat lips
Africa wide hips
Africa perms
Africa conks
Africa bleach
Africa, put powder on
Africa, take those beads off your neck
Africa, take off your kente
Africa, take that head wrap off
Africa, loosen those braids
Africa, cut those locks
Africa, wear silky hair
Africa, use a straightening comb
Africa look like Europe
Africa look like Beauty
Africa, close your eyes
Africa, open your green eyes.
Africa, open your blue eyes.
Africa, open your gray eyes.
Africa, see you in Europe's mirror!
Africa, it is deceit!

CIRCLE OF LIFE

Somewhere between the zeal of the young
and the wisdom of the old
lingers life.
It is first spent crawling on four legs
then walking with two legs
then shuffling with three.

Imagine a fruit tree in the center of a garden.
Fruits may never bear its deep orange and red cloaks,
green the fruits may forever be.
Some may argue
it is all about these moments
when the flesh of the fruit is taut and firm.
The vitality.
Those days spent as green fruits attached to pliable branches
that bend and twist and turn like young ones on a jungle gym.
Or like a young adult
who searches for self
down winding roads where the brush around the bend remains unseen.

I'd rather say it's about the moments that took your breath away—
when the flesh is plush and supple with the juices of experience
the days when fruits are ripe;
the moment before we detach from this branch of life
because that is the time of recollection.
It is when experience's roots pull water from grounds of many
yesterdays—
a time we can remember when so many fruits from all different branches
shared life,
shared raindrops and shared sunlight from above.
Weathered the storms,
survived the chills,
held on to life even when gusts blew with such gusto and force.

We reflect to the day when we were merely seeds in the earth,
appreciate it all
and prepare for the day when we will all be seeds of this earth once
again.

A BLIND MAN'S FAITH

I saw a blind man walking yesterday
so confident of his next step.
He walked a straighter path than a gymnast on a tightrope.
He walks in the dark;
many times I struggle to walk in the light.
Perplexed it may seem,
but sometimes vision is beyond the retina.
It exists in the souls of courage, direction, and faith.
I ponder what it takes to truly walk in confidence
when a veil covers your eyes?

I want to walk with the courage of a blind man.
Unsure of what life offers in his next step
but taking a leap of faith EVERY step I take.

His surroundings remain visually absent
but he FEELS life
with an unequivocal belief
that his future will come into existence,
step by step

He sees the light despite the darkness.
If only I could walk in the dark
with certainty that luminous rays will always light my path.

If only I could possess a blind man's faith.

Ole Charlie Thoreau

Charlie, Charlie, Charlie.
you know I can't forget you,
with a heart of gold,
and a schnauzer like a baby elephant.
The humor you had,
the jokes you told,
your wrinkled countenance,
your honest smile,
the charmed flair you possessed,
the young ladies you flirted with
knowing they'd give you a heart attack.
You didn't care,
you enjoyed life without boundaries,
even if it was from a seated view of a wheelchair.
When I'd stand you up to walk,
you'd shuffle your feet like a deck of cards.
Scared you were,
but me you trusted.
Remember when you told me you couldn't walk anymore?
and I'd say, "Don't you want to waltz with your wife again?"
Boy you'd laugh
and sometimes snort.
A natural happiness I noticed in you,
despite your tremors that Parkinson's gave ya,
you always were on beat to the rhythm of happiness.
Now I know you and your family always thanked me for the care I gave,
but I'd just like to thank you one last time for the laughter you gave.

That good ole Charlie Thoreau.
"Shuffle those feet and foxtrot for the ladies, Charlie!
C'mon now!
And a one!
And a two!
Yeah!"

IN THE NIGHT

Thieving in the dark of the night,
I take grapes of wrath from the vine
crushing pungent decaying fruits
until juices stain my feet
producing wines which travel down passages
to reside in the belly of opportunity.
Create drunken stupors in the mind of you,
since you and they
fathom failure in flawed futures.

Thieving in the night of stolen dreams
to take back what is mine,
breathing life into still bodies of hope,
assembling armies of motive,
unsheathing passion filled swords
and sprinting to the thick of the mess;
slicing bellies of gluttony and greed
and spilling life back onto the earth
so trees of wealth can grow in our communities
and not in foreign lands
that manifest our material weakness
into their monetary gain.

Thieving in the night of hatred,
to rescue love from her captors
infidelity and abhorrence.
Replenish vitality to her once succulent lips
kiss her with such fervor that an oasis is created in the desert.

Thieving in the night of tomorrow—
despite it not being here
because to envision tomorrow
is to first change today.
So call me a thief of time
because I'm stealing the seconds, minutes, and hours
that takes one's breath away
to affect the world in such ways
that douse infernos in hell
and burn oils of frankincense and myrrh in heaven.

RAINBOW

A rainbow appeared outside a little girl's window.
She exclaimed, "I want to go to the top and slide down!
Mommy, may I ride the rainbow?"

Mommy said, "Yes, baby, you can.
Put your hands in the air,
give a grin—that makes the sun yearn for shade
and laugh! Just laugh I tell you!"

The little one smiled, but with a hint of trepidation.
"How do I get up there, Mommy?"
Mommy replied, "Reach to the sky and close your eyes.
You can go wherever you want."
When the little girl complied;
she felt hands hold her hands,
and she soared through the skies and never let go.

Now as a woman of her own
who has accomplished great feats,
many ask her how she had done so well in life.
She looked at her palms
and saw they were still lightly red from the warmth of His loving touch.
She just smiled and gave inaudible thanks.

Years later, she saw a rainbow peeking beyond the clouds
and her little daughter now asked,
"Mommy, may I ride the rainbow?"
Mommy smiled and said, "Yes, dear, reach to the sky
and He will come to you!"

Mansions on Street Corners

Tears of the girl who lives above

quenches the thirst of the man who lives below
right beside the fire in the trash can in the winter.
Her worries are joys he can only dream of.

BLESSED

Blessed are the days that make the heart warm,
the memories fond,
and the future bright.
My words are my window,
and if hardship is my shadow,
then hope is my sunshine.

FORGOTTEN ROSES

Hard liquor he sips
elevating to what life once was.
Lighting the blunt to find the space
between opportunity and fate,
he plucks the ashes and they travel down Fourteenth street.
The sweet stench of the bud
masks the scent of roses in the crevices of the concrete.
People trample these precious flowers
and look above for answers
when perplexing questions are below the line of sight.

A little lower,
deep down in the slums that some call homes exists
a homeless man's mansion,
a dope boy's crack house,
a dealer's revenue,
and a jail system's jackpot.

You hear the sirens
and pull to the side of the road,
but have the courage to stand in the center of the road!
Hands clasped praying,
tandem walking on yellow lines,
a steady pace to selflessness.

Have empathy for their tears
and our mourning streets
There is no rain to wash away the pains,
just misfortune in an empty Thunderbird bottle.

Today, shine light on these roses.
Pick one up,
breathe life into it,
take captives of poverty from the depths of the streets
to the heights of our love.
Their progression should be our mission.

"Service is the rent we pay for living."
Word to Marian Wright Edelman.

GOOD MORNING, METROPOLIS

Good morning, metropolis.
Caramel-scented mocha and shots of espresso fill my nostrils,
skyscrapers scrape the skies of a city awakening from a night under
the stars.
Men in tailored business suits brush off their lapels,
throw leather bags over shoulder
and power walk to buses, trains and Mercedes.
Women of the same caliber
walk with subtle confidence ready to tackle boardrooms
and prove themselves as equal or often better counterparts.
Health care professionals button their lab coats,
students from all disciplines turn on their iPods
and travel wherever their morning's musical journeys take them.
Smartphone screens light up,
morning news and social networks are browsed,
prayers for the day are sent up to the Most High
while swears are uttered under some breaths
because they can't remember the last day they had off.
Public transportation fill the near silence of a city that has yet another
day in front of it,
Another day has begun . . .
Good morning, metropolis.

TRANSCENDENTALIST PERSPECTIVE

At the frantic pace of a butterfly's wings,
I remain above,
a few inches above the treetops,
but so far away from the stars.
I look above every night from the surface as if they're within my grasp,
yet my tears create the depth of oceans
and I paddle through emotion's waters
toward the horizon as if the answer is there,
but it's only a mirage.

In my better moods
my blessings illuminate the earth and
success brings sun rays;
however, some still prefer the shade,
the cool in the calamity of the content
in the hills where things remain to be seen.

I stand on the other side
seeing what they cannot from a bird's-eye view
and through the multifaceted lens of creatures that roam on more
than two legs.
Life is seen,
through a score of perspectives.
Variety of many becomes diversity of one,
in relation and uncommon at the same time,
paradoxical like rain and sun simultaneously.
This is spontaneously despicable love and amicable anger,
futile strength and inexpressible expression,
mute dialect.
Life is stuck somewhere between tomorrow and infinity
and truth and illusion,
smiles and ulterior motives,
breath and stillness
and friend and foe.

Like a butterfly who appears to be liberated,
I remain in balance between the earth and the skies.
So like the grounded man I am,
I sit on nature's bed of grass and look above for answers to it all.

I Ain't Got It

If it ain't the 1st or the 15th,
then it ain't but an object that eludes
the palms of the hands,
but transforms into ink on dotted lines
and into tidbits of information
traveling through a wire worth the wealth of a nation
that's only a bounced check away from the year of 1929.

DELAYED APPRECIATION

I want to change,
but the pennies in my pocket slipped through worn holes.
It seems that every since I spent my last cent,
I've been searching far and near for what always lied in the palm of my
hand as well as discarded on the sidewalks.
Perhaps if I had realized
that a plethora of smaller, lesser things
can accrue to gems of such great value,
I may be just a little better off.

CHARITY

The most beautiful image in the world
is not the sun at the break of dawn
nor the moon shining radiant in an opaque sky.
It is not the glimmer of gold and riches
discovered in a wooden chest
nor is it the architecture of skyscrapers
amongst the silhouette of a city.
It is the image of humanity's charity—
the interlocked fingers of love
all colors of mankind meshing to form rainbows
after the storms.
We stand together
with the bright rays of God shining down on us.
To help others is to help oneself be the best he or she can be.
His tears are our tears;
Her joy is our happiness.
Charity.

SKELETON KEYS

Homeless man, please lend me your keys.
I've lived behind this door far too long
in rooms of empty gratitude.
I am not thankful enough.
I throw away my leftovers while you find meals in trash cans,
I dress in expensive clothes
while you wear ragged sweaters in the summer
and shoes with holes in the soles while you walk in the snow.
I sleep in a bed with plush linen
and you lay on newspapers on park benches.

You see, it's the simple things I don't appreciate!
Like I have my own private bathroom,
but you defecate in hidden alleys
and urinate on barren soil.
I shower every morning,
yet your body reeks of strife and turmoil.
I am not thankful!

Lend me your keys.
For I have lived behind this door for too long.
This door has protected me;
yet has blinded from understanding real hardship.
I fail to understand my own blessings;
yet if I possessed your eyesight,
I would realize that I live in great splendor.

You live in the darkness of society.
I wonder, do you see the light?
Do you see what the insect in the grass sees
or what the eagle sees when it soars above?

Homeless man, lend me your keys
for you unlock doors of honest and bare perspective.
If I could fathom your pain,
then I could appreciate the breath in my lungs,
the riches in my hand,
and the blessings of my soul.

SIBAHLE'S ARABESQUE

A silhouette elegant like a swan mimics her movements of grace.
The sun brings light to the flame of her dreams as
she dances amidst a background of shanty houses.
She effortlessly ascends in the air as if wind is the ground she walks
on.

A South African beauty frolics on the idea of hope,
even in the midst of defeat
her desire is ethereal,
across seas and vast lands others spot her flame and beckon to it.

When her flame flickered in the eye of the storm,
a kind heart gave it life again
so that her dream of dancing may release her and others
from the captivity of poverty.

Her dance is such a brave interpretation of courage.
Sibahle's Arabesque.

EXCEPTIONAL MEN

To stand grounded
but to soar
is paradox of concrete thought
yet blissful to great minds.
It is the rationale of courage
and the courage of morality.
In murals of humane artistry,
it is the definitive stroke of life—
the captivation of life's fine details.
Life's desire
to no longer close eyes and dream
but to achieve.
To possess unshackled vision
and to take life with labored hands.
To smash Berlin walls with bare fists,
to extinguish fires in Kenyan churches,
to walk down Piru street and not bear arms,
but embrace troubled brothers in open arms.
It is to live with the faith of Martin,
the compassion of Gandhi.
the fire of Malcolm,
and the heart of God.
To live the lives of exceptional men!

MARTYRS

If today was January 30, 1948,
If today was February 21, 1965,
If today was April 4, 1968,
I would discard bullets before fiery discharges
so heroes wouldn't have to die as martyrs.

TIME

In my life,
I would grab the second hand of the world's most grandiose grandfather
clock and ride it like a rollercoaster,
catapult into the skies of carpe diem
and grab a faraway star.

I would look into retrospect's eyes and
see no tears of regret.
When perspective sought clarity,
my vision would be pristine
because experience is life's biography.

I intend to tell the story of a gentle man
with insurmountable strength and courage,
who forged paths across many vistas
on firm ground
and through the quicksand,
down smooth dirt roads flanked with beautiful orchids
and through passages that seemed more like barriers
with their entanglements of branches and entrapping vines.

I pray that time's concerto is harmonious
and my heart will beat to the tempo of a life laden in great experiences.

THORNS OF ROSES

Demented by her beauty,
morning dew on her petals,
he lewdly strokes her body with—fingers
and leaves blood on her stems.
She doesn't want to be uprooted from her fertile soil,
placed in foreign grounds
or a vase in a room to be looked upon.
She doesn't want her petals to be removed
slowly and seductively
nor abruptly
nor frantically
because it'll leave her insecurities naked.
She says—
"Don't touch me there,
don't rub me,
don't grope me,
don't abuse me.
Don't clip my stems and place them in rubbish.
The water of life exists in my stems
nourished from the soil I grew in.
Don't snatch me away from my virginal roots
before I even have the chance to blossom
or you'll leave blood all over my stems—
difficult to distinguish
if it is mine or yours—
these will be stained memories
that raindrops will never wash away."

SAKEINEH MOHAMMADI ASHTIANI

Before I rest my eyes at night, I pray for Sakeineh.
I pray for her young son.
May he embrace his mother
in the calm of life away from the calamity of her government.

They wish to bury her in the sand and cast stones,
hurl accusations at her face
until tears moisten barren sands
and her sacrifice paints the ground a new color.

The sin of adultery she supposedly committed
and she should die a dishonorable death as stated by the men of her
government.
I wish to save her and release the bird from its cage
for she deserves to fly free of fear
of men who think they hold her fate in the palms of their gritty hands.

Sack of Coins

Grandma gave me a sack of coins
when I was 'ye high.
Wealth in a bag and
love in the heart.
Weekly trips to the sickly,
put humility and the necessity of service in the palms of my hands.

Runnin' red lights,
speeding down the highway
on the way downtown
with me in the backseat,
gave me a daring spirit.

Salmon patties, rice, butter beans, and okra,
fried chicken and yams,
mason jars of peaches, apricots, and pears stored for the winter.
Blueberries and muscadines in the fall—
pickin' 'em,
puttin' 'em in the bucket.
Pound cakes and fruit cakes weekly
for the visitors
because everyone was treated as family when they entered Grandma's
house.
This is how hospitality entered my soul.

Grandma gave me a sack of coins when I was 'ye high,
wealth in a bag I tell ya,
Just this mornin'
after life had added a few more layers and a little more wisdom,
I looked in the bedroom where I rested my head as a boy
and I discovered my wealth once again.
I realized it never left me,
So when I have a family of my own,
her tradition will remain with me—
and it all started with a sack of coins.

EN FLIGHT TO EXODUS
(IN MEMORY OF YAGUINE KOITA
AND FODE TOUNKAR)

Airplanes with the wings of hope
above the clouds of poverty and
monochrome landscapes,
bring Yimabaya to tears.

These tears turn dirt to mud
that sticks in the crevices of young boys' sandals.
They step on soil rich with minerals yet, void of wealth.
They pray for freedom from poverty
and dream in the undercarriages of opportunity.

Engines roar through the cold skies,
tears frozen on young faces
and breath is sequestered from life.
A letter lives on
asking the world to dry the tears of Yimabaya.

Mother Africa breast-fed humanity in the youth of time,
now reciprocation of love and nourishment is longed for.
Two young boys
no longer have the privilege to dream at night.
Their ascension occurred before their exodus.
May their souls rest in peace.

FOR YOU

For you I pray that love descends from heavenly skies
to arrive within the depths of your heart.

For you I pray that birds sing an angel's song outside your window
to awaken strength and reverence in your heart in the morning of
mourning.

For you I wish I could bear the weight of your sorrow on my shoulders,
so this burden you would not have to carry alone.

For you I wish I could summon a summer breeze to dry your eyes
or part the clouds after a wintry storm to dissipate your tears.

For you I wish I could give flowers that could emulate the beauty of your
mother's spirit,
but I'm convinced her presence made roses bloom and sequoias
sprout.

Just remember there are rainbows after the storm—
and those rainbows are in your heart.
So continue to live because the light that shines in your soul is no longer
just yours,
God and your mother's radiance also shines bright in you.

WIND OF LIFE

May my words be the wind
that turns pages in the moment of experience.
At night I see beacons
that guide me to sunrise.
Like the sea,
my heart holds treasures.
Like flat land,
my discipline is level.
Similar to the air currents,
my presence is always felt;
you can see the way my love affects God's creations,
it is gentle and serene.
Just look at how the trees sway to my emotion
and fallen leaves dance on the ground
invigorated with life again.
They travel back to their branches
and change from darkened colors to lively green hues.
They speak new life;
love is life
and life is love.

My words are the wind
that turns pages in the moment of experience.

BRAVEHEART

In a world without courage,
rats gallivant and lions cower,
mice stomp the earth and elephants scurry,
buzzards soar and eagles merely fly,
snakes walk upright and men crawl.
The sun doesn't shine,
nor do the stars glisten at night.
Fresh water is thick and vile.
The scent of flowers is pungent.
The sins of the unjust pollute the air.
Human bile, lymph, and pus of the body
ascend in arteries to the heart of justice.
Necrosis of hope,
suffocation and infarctions lay souls to rest.

But to speak and act in truth
is to fertilize the earth.
To exhibit moral value and humane decency
is to turn young sprouts to sequoias.
To act with dignity
is to bring nourishing showers to the land.
To give love
is to blossom as flowers.
To show courage
is to thrust spears from the highest mountaintop
to pierce the bodies of fallacy.
To show valiance
is to smack gavels on Injustice's head
with such force
that glaciers in the Arctic split
and justice is liberated.

Now this is a world I want to live in.
May my soul never inhale in cowardice.
May I live to become a **BRAVEHEART.**

SECTION II

THE METRONOME OF LOVE AND MUSIC

Moments in love just might bloom all roses in sight.

He would travel miles and miles in a caravan
filled with brass and memories.

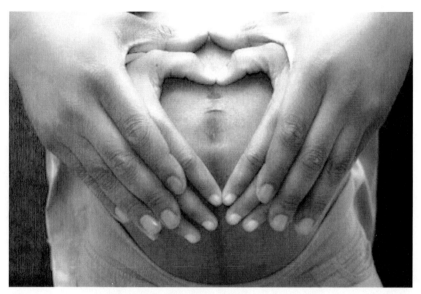

One mind. One soul. One heart. Union.

It's her beach I dream of being stranded on.

His heart still pulsates to the memory of music.

INFINITELY BEAUTIFUL

You are beautiful.
Simply beautiful;
Yet it's complex to figure how God created you with such finesse.
I swear, beauty was birthed in your smile,
beautiful like the sun's rays dancing on the morning ocean
beautiful like the moon's glow on a star—filled night
beautiful like birds singing sweet songs amongst treetops
beautiful like something I've never witnessed before—
like a blind man standing before architecture of Italy
just unheard of
like a deaf man walking past a street musician
on the corner of Beethoven and Coltrane
or Mozart and Ellington.

Truthfully, there are no words to express
but still I delve into seas of vernacular,
spew out geysers of lexicon,
run across fields of syntax
in hope to design sentences
to explain how I feel about you.
I just want to fall asleep in your glow
and wake up in your radiance;
breathe in your beauty's euphoria
and never exhale
just to keep your air inside of me
and if I must exhale
let me exhale in flowing verse,
speaking in unfamiliar tongue, babbling in Eros's language,
expressing my emotions one by one
with space in staccato sectioned in sweet syllables
or fluid like rain showers,
water dripping down from leaf to leaf
filling cupped hands 'til they runneth over
just to take a sip of your beauty.

I'm high off your beauty like
I look into eagle eyes
or drunk like Dionysus just yelled,
"All drinks on me!"
I could write about your beauty forever,
like my ink is ethereal
lighting up fire in script.
Feelings burning wildly on propane pads
combusting in eruptions when memory recalls your eyes' seduction.
You make my rhythm incoherent—
Discombobulated.

Gregory Hines can't tap into my reservoir of emotion.
Flappers and jazzy men can't step to my heartbeat when I see you.
You can flip quarters in ol' skool jukeboxes,
selection to selection but,
the Spinners can't spin my weaves of love.
The Whispers whisper sweet nothings in comparison to my lovesick
declarations.
The Temptations can't harmonize notes nor synchronize steps
to my melodies when I see you . . .
and if they tried they'd sing in crazed chords and stumble all over mic
cords trying to express the beauty of you.

I could ramble on forever and forever about you!
I mean, rap a minute past tomorrow about you,
bask in your ambience and live
from saved soul to saved soul past eternity,
exist in the moment between last breath and first gasp of air,
the moment between eye contact and love at first sight,
the moment between "Ummm, I kind of like you" and "Girl, I want you to
be mine."

Linger in the split second between p.m. and a.m.
and write until the sun comes up
then write until a.m. greets p.m.
Grab some more paper and do it all over again.

I could really go on forever,
but to make a long story short,
I'd just like to say,
"I think you are so beautiful . . ."

LET'S STAY IN

Guitar strings
and symphonies of words
candlelit dinner
aged red wine
then sweet strawberries in her mouth
and rose petals under her feet
make a romantic evening.
Love while the candle burns
and the hot wax drips
and she's speechless—
motionless.
There she falls asleep in my arms,
in love
we lie.

DON'T LET MY LOVE SLIP AWAY

Don't let these bombs burst in the air
before my heart has the chance to explode
sparkles and flames everywhere—
the envy of the stars.

My love shall radiate for you.
Don't let this oil mask the oceans
before I have the chance to kiss you under waterfalls.
Don't let this market crash
before I have the chance to crash and burn
in your passionate inferno.

Don't let these politicians reverse humanity's progress
before love's future finds itself in the palms of the present.
Don't let my love slip away in these times of society
despite danger and chaos in this world.
My life is in worse jeopardy without you,
so I wait to embrace you for the first time
for that will be the moment when my exhalations
are the air that soothes the misogyny of mankind.

AND IF I FALL

I just want to fall in love
and if I ever fall out of love,
let me plummet from the skies
only to fall back into your warm embrace.
In my descent to your heaven
from high skies,
I will ride on passion's wings
to arrive at the kiss of your lips.
When lips part,
speak no words,
just love.
Yes. Just . . . love.

THIS DESIRE

Greeks talk of Aphrodite.
The Yoruba people speak of Oshun.
According to folklore,
they both possess an enigma of the same—
to receive their tokens.
I'd give them anything,
ambrosia for her
or garments with yellow hues turned white again for the other.

LOVE JONES

Getting my Darius Lovehall on,
wondering if Nina is in the vicinity—
so cleverly elusive to me
like trails of cigar smoke.

Words from the wordsmith ease into the air.
Someone plucks the strings of the bass,
the trumpeter plays a song of the Sirens
luring me to her.
I'm hoping the fate the Greeks spoke of was truly a myth
because I can't resist.
Her ambience is the air I want to breathe.
Whispering her heart's desire in my ear
to the rhythm of Charlie Parker's black-and-white notes or sumthin,'
her words now dance in my mind
to the beats from the stage—
rhythm of the Congo drum:
boom, boom, bap, boom, boom, boom, boom, bap
boom, boom, bap, boom, boom, boom, boom, bap.

Her features are heirlooms of African ancestry.
Her head wrap offers a glimpse of her curly hair.
Her sensuous movements leave scents of jojoba oil.
Almond-shaped eyes
succulent lips
skin so beautiful
must've been heaven's canvas.
An angel's flawless painting
comes to life with her presence.
Dialogues of introduction pursue.
She has dreams of a PhD,
two kids, maybe three—
waiting for her husband-to-be.

Romance persuade her heart's lock to dangle the keys,
I remind her candlelight dinners.
Sweet with sounds of Ledisi can be
reality on imagination's wings.

She closes her eyes
as we slow dance.
She asks me, "When I open my eyes, will this be just a memory?"
I hold her closer . . .
and whisper,
"A memoir sketched in elegant cursive—
the ink hasn't yet dried
only the first sentences have been written.
Let's write this love story together."

THUS SPAKE LOVE

If I can move mountains with my faith,
I wonder, can I move your world with my love?
May I skip these pebbles of interest across your pond?
If my words sink in your waters,
let them plummet to the depths of your heart.
If a chasm exists behind your ribs,
let my affection replenish your emptiness.
May my passion be your conduits?
I promise my electricity will awaken your excitement.
When you close your eyes,
I am your dream of a tropical paradise . . .
and when you open your eyes.
I am the rare black sand beneath your feet
and the sparkling blue waters and crimson sun at your horizon.
I am your mirage and your reality.
Let's dance on this thin line of fantasy and truth.
Our love can give off flares hotter than the sun.
It was at the speed of a comet
that I fell for you;
we are written in the stars above.
So may you no longer ignore the glistening stars above us.
My soul shines bright when I look into eyes,
So answer my request from the courage of love and not from the fear
of past relationships.
Just say yes . . .
Just. Say. Yes.

INTOXICATION

Kicks and a snare,
her heartbeat is my bass.
Like Narcissus
she sees her reflection
but in a drink the color of Egyptian riches.
Golden ink.
Dark, smooth, and strong.

She tastes it,
velvet plush lips
twist to the curvature of the glass—
cranberry colors.
Red wine paints her soul the color of red roses.
She drinks—

Vodka on the rocks.
The ice in her glass slowly descends
like rocks after skipping the face of a pond.

Champagne is her vice
bubbles from her beverage,
rise like dew after the break of dawn.

Her last mojito hints at her mood—
vibrant with color and full of life for the night.
It is my golden ink she drinks
intoxicated
punch drunk love—
the liquor of lust—
Pleasure.

DECEIT OF EROS?

Standing over her balcony
looking into the depths for something
Eros is sound asleep in her satin sheets,
but I wish to wake Agape.
I want to define love in her eyes—
an unequivocal love that supersedes passion without hearts.
Benevolent and selfless,
I will cater to her,
serve her platters of respect and care;
offer her Spanish red wines.

My sacrifice to her
is me,
so I turn from the balcony,
away from my thoughts and back to her bedroom.
I awaken Eros from her slumber
and like singers sing ballads
and dancers dance nights away,
we make love.
Like lovers in lust in search of what is deeper—
two souls intertwining in Agape's union,
in the presence of what many search lifetimes for.
Nevertheless, we . . .
and again,
and again.
Victims of lust
or victors of love?

Bittersweet,
Eros or Agape?
Which one are you, my love?

LUST

Like Adams orbiting around the physics of her.
like atoms dancing in the energy of Eden.
On the Eve of temptation,
on the Eve of sin
and somewhere between the dusk of moonlight
and the dawn of the sun,
men bite worm-riddled apples.

LOVER'S ASCENSION

If I could pluck a dahlia from the rolling hills of West Virginia
and place it behind her ear while
whispering sweet nothings to her,
my words blending with nature's gentle hush.
I'd kiss her in a California summer rain,
be her warmth in Ann Arbor's chill,
dive with her into waters of Carolina,
free fall from the clouds,
dance on a rainbow after the storm,
touch the top of a Palmetto,
make love under waterfalls,
massage her feet with lavender,
listen to her rhythmic heart songs,
lay on a medley of flower petals,
climb mountains of passion,
experience volcanic eruptions of love,
cherishing her endlessly—
no horizons in sight.

Our love will ascend before the morning's dew is dry
and travel to the heavens once the sun sets in the west.

My love.

LOVE

Rain blossoms flowers;
Dry and arid grounds leave them lifeless.
With that being said,
I don't want to love less.
I'd rather let love shower down on me
a small drizzle,
or a constant monsoon, or
whatever the case may be
so I can say I enjoyed the moments.
Even when times turn harsh
and the land is barren
and the beauty of love is unseen
when love is nothing more
than a hushed breeze that barely moves a rose's petal,
I can say it was better to love and have lost
than to never have loved at all.

TEARS AT SEA

If I cast the bucket to the bottom of the well and it is without water, then I shall dive in oceans in search of your last tear of joy to quench my thirst.

Unrequited Love

He closes his eyes and remembers her.
He sits on a stool
old wooden floors crick with his every move.
Chandeliers glimmer through the haze.
The ivories usher Für Elise into the air
humble smells of antiquity
ease him into rustic yesterdays.

He remembers her in Picasso's fragmented artistry
like a picturesque imagination to a canvas.
He was drawn,
in awe of her beauty.
He was captivated,
but she was never his to be.
Her heart was already crafted,
sketched on another's canvas
before his paint dried.
Love's easel he would've supported her with;
Instead, she stood against the backdrop
of off-white walls and chipping paint.
This love could've been
more beautiful than the ceilings of the Sistine chapel!

She left his heart's complexities residing in Van Gogh's realm
and like his art, the world ignored.
His care was unseen by her
posthumous recognition will be useless
because his heart has died loveless.

However with demise, something anew comes to rise.
Even dead plants prepare the soil for more life.
A lover's resuscitation rekindles life.
Blood flows through vessels, ventricles, and atriums
as he dips his paintbrush into the water
to dissolve old, crusted paint.

Life is revived
with colors matching the reincarnation of springtime.
He awaits the moment to sketch a new beauty,
one that will allow him to detail her intricacies
da Vinci her uniqueness
and give her love . . . life
Eternal in the stroke of his brush.

ESCAPING SANDS

Time, not seized, is like waves at the shore
and sands escape to the sea.
Emotions are sometimes lost
and the sands may never reach the shore again.
Feelings never expressed
remain lost treasures at sea.
If the breeze rides the cusp of the ocean waves
then may your hands form seashells
so the sands may never escape
like a pearl in a clam
love exists within.
Footprints of faith are in the sand,
and I am living in your moment.

APRIL'S JOY

It's a beautiful day so let's enjoy the sun.
We sit out on the grass
with the squirrels climbing trees
and searching for nuts.
Butterflies dance in the rhythm of the wind
and we lie in nature's arms
eating sandwiches and chocolate chip cookies.
We reminisce and dream in one breath,
eyes meet and souls follow soon after.
Smiles after smile
comfort in camaraderie,
our backs to each other we scribble scripts
from our stream of consciousnesses.
Giggly like lil' children—
shy to divulge—
I finally read my words.
She reads hers.
She's certain that I won't like it,
but I do.
I appreciate her intellect and creativity all in one
I can't help but smile as her
poetry sprouts like the blades of grass we lay on.
Next comes the raindrops.
I wrap her in a blanket and put my arms around her,
amazed by her tranquil beauty inside and out.
I am captivated by the poetry of her spirit;
her pentameters
are the beat to my heart.
Her poetic license
is my stream of happiness.
She makes me smile.
She is my poetry in motion.

SOAKING UP THE SUN

Girl you are soaking up the sun!
You say, "Mornings are a tease for the light;
and evenings are reminders
that all that descends will RISE again!"
You say, "Rains pour from my eyes when clouds form,
but the bright, blue skies are my soul after a terrible storm."

Your smile is life for flowers and children of the spring
when the sun is in hiding.
Your petals hold the dew of yesterday's joys.
I admire the way you live your life,
so lush with the warmth of good times.
I just want to bask in your rays
and live off of your happiness.
Yes!

EVER AGAIN

I hope that if I ever write a poem about her again,
it will have no commas nor will it end in a period.
My words will be my breath.
My life shall be eternal,
for I may never cease
to explore words
that explain the love I have for her.

King

An opportunity to him is like a flame in the dark,
but a gift to her is like a flame amidst sunrays.
He walks on shards of glass,
she walks on gold.
He lives in a hut;
she, a mansion.
He's a king in tattered garments.
She looks outside her window
past the oak trees, fruit trees, and manicured gardens
and sees only his torn garments.

SOUL SISTA

The sun filters through dusty windows.
We ride by rustic buildings,
gritty brownstones,
and parks with lifeless plants and
roads littered with potholes;
yet I can't help but to gaze at her hair—
natural curls bounce as we ride through the city streets,
and her natural curves peak from behind bus seats.
The silver rail which she holds onto is firm,
but her posture is stronger;
Yet she is so delicate.
Like rain to soil,
her skin is softened by essential oils;
her presence is essential to my being.

Soul sista,
as we sit on this bus after our nine to fives
or late afternoon chemistry classes,
I hope our chemistry crashes
like waves onto the shore.

It is her beach I dream of being stranded on.
It is her heartbeat that I find the sweetest melody.
Soul sista you are.

Black women,
I respect appreciate, desire, need, and yearn for you
Black women, I love you all.

AFFIRMATION

When opposite isn't always the opposition
and friends frown at night
and smile in the day,
love is the same.
We only shift our perception of it.
Thus, we find rocks,
treasure them for a lifetime.
Discover jewels,
love them for a day
then throw them back into the dirt,
as if love has failed.

Until our perception of love aligns with the love of God
we are only lost in love and not secure in it.

MUSIC IS NOISE

Sweet melodies she hears no more.
She finds solace in the cacophony of broken strings
and madness in silence.
Music is noise.
Her heart beats to arrhythmias—
erratic like heavy teardrops falling on sixty-six keys—
making noise from a heart that once produced love refrains.
When distinction between harmonies fades,
Sharps, flats, and skewed keys,
rusted brass,
cracked reeds,
and leaky valves
create her sound.

Her heart beats to heartbreak
and she says she is fine with this
as long as she never has to perform solos
amidst bright lights that exposes her soul.
So she performs under dim lights of a man
who doesn't value the beauty of her melody . . .
she is out of tune with love.

IF I COULD SING

If I could sing
I'd sing you something in A-minor—
make your heartbeat flutter to volatile scats,
serenade you with testimonies of my love for you,
allow chromatic escapades to ascend in steps
to your bedroom,
experience sixteenths and eighths
as our eyes met.
Let the whole, half, and quarter notes
tell our story in a most beautiful harmony—
an étude for lovers.
A template for love
transcends conditions—
a paradigm for happiness.

Let my fingers dance on your keys;
sweet music we will make.

In A-minor I would sing;
to you, I'd bring ballads to existence.
We'd make love to music
and music with love.

"Sweet—doodle la-we-bop
la-do-a-we baby
you make me so crazy,
in love you leave me sugar.
Moments in love just might,
bloom all roses in sight.
Be with me tonight
and the morning thereafter
and love me 'til infinity."
The band plays on.

If I could sing, I'd swear I sing to you in A-minor—
nights in Harlem
the roaring twenties we'd go—
letting the music take us for the entire show.

MEMORY OF MUSIC

Deaf with a soul bright like a summer holiday,
he listens with eyes bright
just so he can feel the band.
He would travel miles and miles in a caravan filled with brass and
memories to feel the warmth in the Coltrane.
Riding on tracks that brings him to dizzying spells—
caught in a rapture.
Intertwined in a melodious bliss of raindrops
as they irresistibly tap on his window.

The duke of rhythm
ushers him into a life where trumpets awaken creation
yet he is deaf in a room of instruments,
but alive when fingers press valves and caress keys
and cradle drumsticks.
Black-and-white photos of the soul become vibrant in the color of
rhythm.
The mute of the horn uncovers passion and life.
The music in his soul shall never be silenced
even if his ears no longer brings lexicons of sheet music to auditory
life.
His heart still pulsates to the memory of music.
His eyes relive what he no longer hears,
he sees their finger snaps and foot stomps.
Head nods and hand claps.
This is his metronome
as he plays into the sultry air.

VINYL

I will play tomorrow's song on an old '45.
Put life under the needle,
guide through the grooves of the past,
and recapture the classic wisdom of vintage.
Vintage understanding.
Bebop in reverie's humble cot,
hip-hop in experience's full lot,
spin records in ole music shops.

GRAFFITI ON THE WALLS

Fresh out of the inner city's womb,
the intricacies are intertwined,
twisting down fallopian tubes
to a place where the youth carry textbooks in their arms
and boom boxes over their shoulders.
Young adults hip-hop in phone booths
to unbutton white collars and become b-boys
listening to hip-hop while deciphering anatomies of the world.
Seeking to understand origins
because insertions elsewhere in life sometimes makes one forget
how culture came before the business.

Make concentric moves against the gravity of society's disapproval.
Elevate to the top of Planet Rock.
View life from mountains on Digable Planets.
Break dance on sidewalks,
scratch on the ones and twos.
kick rhymes on the microphone.

Tell Roxanne I didn't mean those silly things.
Let's work it out.
She can be my lyric to life.
It will be fresh like the prince.
Blast "Paul Revere" or "The Bridge Is Over"
on the elite side of town.
Let the decibels shatter glass houses and
tag white picket fences that guard close-minded thoughts.
Grab more spray cans and create pictures of the hip-hop greats.

In the sage's pages this may never be mentioned,
so give Basquiat eternity.
Light ethereal flames in old trash cans
to illuminate the art on the backdrop of gritty bricks and old stones
watch humanity gather around and rub cold hands
and make minds warmer
all on the block and in the alleyways of mental processes.

It is written on the wall and do you want to know what it says?
"I will forever love hip-hop."

'64 Blues House

'64 blues house.
Dizzy, Duke, Miles.
Max Roach protect the art.
Mingus keep the peace alive,
we only want to hear the crickets
and the tiptoeing of the insomniac bass after dark.
Ray Charles give the people sight.
Louie scat down the hatred with your be-bopping ways.
Thelonious Monk, what's up?
Give the world what they need,
for we all can benefit from a little bit of rhythm.
It's all about the jazz, baby.
'64 blues house, baby.
Yeah!

SILHOUETTE BEAUTY

Images of your visage,
The taste of your presence.
So sweet like the honeysuckle of nature.
Desires of an utopian state of bliss.
Still longing for the softness of plush red raspberries,
to engage in a kiss.
Imagine wild and fervent rapids
propelling us into tranquil waters of love.
Waterfalls of happiness crashing onto boulders of joy,
wildly spraying storms of desire onto your kinky hair.
Your skin absorbs the illustrious droplets as your eyes absorb my
deepest thoughts.
As I stare into your eyes, I'm lost in a frantic atmospheric field of Cupid's
most potent arrows.
I am struck.
By your chestnut eyes,
They are like transparent jewels.
I understand your intricacy.
I know why your heart beats to this pattern.

Far from above,
The sun attempts to outshine your radiant glow.
A silhouette is cast,
and it transfuses with the sun's rays.
Your silhouette dances with the waves of the water and your every
movement.
I'm lulled into your world.
I close and reopen my eyes,
praying I'm not lost in a mirage of love.
Our shadows touch, fusing into one.
One mind.
One soul.
One heart.
Union.

My eyes dismiss from the enchanting silhouettes and I lose myself in
your gaze . . .
Under the brilliant sun rays of our best times,
I wake up from my fantasy's stupor.
I look at the ocean,
I look at the skies,
I look at the sands beneath my feet,
and I notice the projection of only my shadow.
Mysteriously I wonder,
Where did my silhouette beauty go?

ABOUT THE AUTHOR

Christopher Gaskins graduated from the University of South Carolina with a Bachelor of Science in Exercise Science and Howard University with a Master of Science in Occupational Therapy. He now lives and works in the Washington D.C. metropolitan area. As an occupational therapist, Gaskins is able to fulfill his desire to help others. He hopes to participate in more humanitarian efforts to aid the impoverished and disadvantaged in the near future.

Edwards Brothers Malloy
Thorofare, NJ USA
April 23, 2012